WELCOME TO THE WORLD OF INFOGRAPHICS

Using icons, graphics and pictograms, infographics visualise information in a whole new way!

READ ABOUT ONE OF THE OLDEST BOARD GAMES IN THE WORLD.

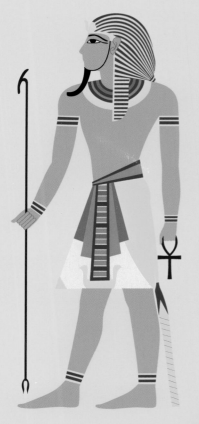

FIND OUT THE WEIGHT OF TUTANKHAMUN'S DEATH MASK.

SEE HOW THE EGYPTIANS USED PICTURES TO MAKE WORDS.

FIND OUT WHAT A PHARAOH WORE AND CARRIED.

COMPARE HOW BIG THE GREAT PYRAMID OF GIZA IS TO MORE MODERN BUILDINGS.

WHO WERE THE EGYPTIANS?

Set along the banks of the River Nile in northern Africa, the Egyptian empire spanned nearly 3,000 years. During that time, its influence spread deep into Africa and the Middle East. Its history is made up of different eras, some in which its power grew, and some when it was conquered and ruled by other people.

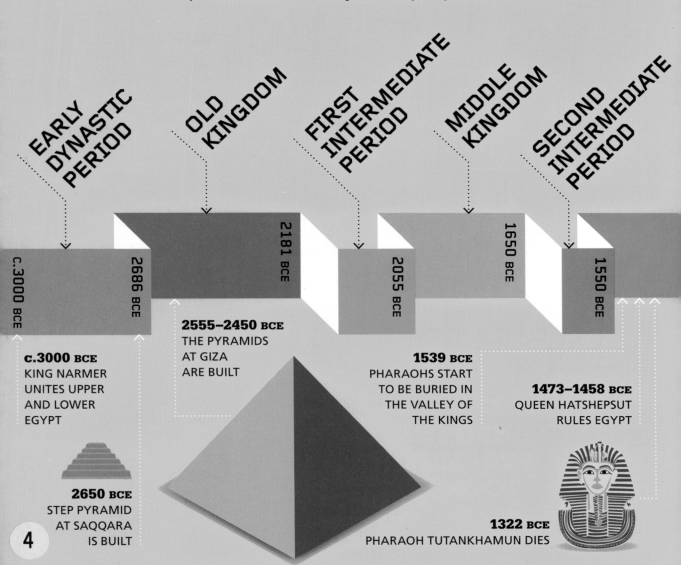

EARLY DYNASTIC PERIOD

OLD KINGDOM

FIRST INTERMEDIATE PERIOD

MIDDLE KINGDOM

SECOND INTERMEDIATE PERIOD

c.3000 BCE

2686 BCE

2181 BCE

2055 BCE

1650 BCE

1550 BCE

c.3000 BCE
KING NARMER UNITES UPPER AND LOWER EGYPT

2555–2450 BCE
THE PYRAMIDS AT GIZA ARE BUILT

2650 BCE
STEP PYRAMID AT SAQQARA IS BUILT

1539 BCE
PHARAOHS START TO BE BURIED IN THE VALLEY OF THE KINGS

1473–1458 BCE
QUEEN HATSHEPSUT RULES EGYPT

1322 BCE
PHARAOH TUTANKHAMUN DIES

THE EGYPTIAN EMPIRE WAS MADE UP OF TWO KINGDOMS – UPPER AND LOWER EGYPT.

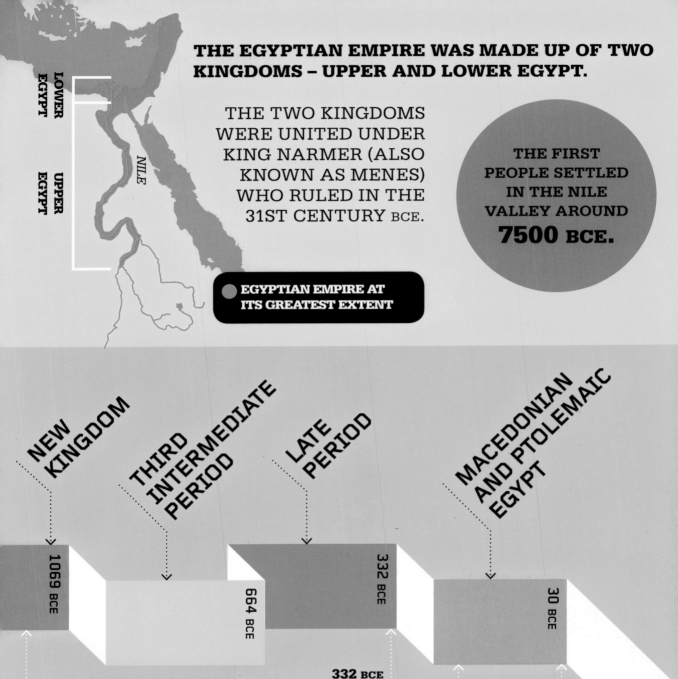

LOWER EGYPT

UPPER EGYPT

NILE

THE TWO KINGDOMS WERE UNITED UNDER KING NARMER (ALSO KNOWN AS MENES) WHO RULED IN THE 31ST CENTURY BCE.

THE FIRST PEOPLE SETTLED IN THE NILE VALLEY AROUND **7500 BCE.**

● EGYPTIAN EMPIRE AT ITS GREATEST EXTENT

NEW KINGDOM

1069 BCE

THIRD INTERMEDIATE PERIOD

664 BCE

LATE PERIOD

332 BCE

MACEDONIAN AND PTOLEMAIC EGYPT

30 BCE

332 BCE
ALEXANDER THE GREAT CONQUERS EGYPT

51–30 BCE
CLEOPATRA, THE LAST PHARAOH, RULES EGYPT

196 BCE
THE ROSETTA STONE IS CARVED

1279–1213 BCE
PHARAOH RAMESSES II RULES EGYPT

THE NILE

The longest river in the world, the Nile was the source of everything for Ancient Egypt, and the main highway connecting both ends of the empire. Its regular flooding provided much-needed nutrients to the soil and decided what happened when during the Egyptian year.

DELTA

The Nile Delta is where the river meets the Mediterranean Sea. One of its biggest ancient cities is Alexandria, founded by Alexander the Great in 331 BCE. Historically, it was home to a huge lighthouse and the Great Library – the largest library in the ancient world.

×100

THE LARGEST BOATS SAILING UP AND DOWN THE NILE COULD EACH CARRY UP TO 500 TONNES OF CROPS AND CARGO – THAT'S MORE THAN THE WEIGHT OF 100 ELEPHANTS!

MEDITERRANEAN SEA

NILE DELTA

ALEXANDRIA

MEMPHIS

was the capital city of Egypt during the Old Kingdom period.

SOBEK

The oasis of Faiyum was the site of the city of Sobek. The Greeks called this place 'Crocodilopolis' because the locals worshipped a sacred crocodile that lived in a pond in one of the city's temples.

THE NILE IS ABOUT

6,650 KILOMETRES

LONG AND DRAINS AN AREA OF SOME

3,349,000

SQUARE KILOMETRES
– MORE THAN

10

PER CENT
OF THE ENTIRE
AFRICAN
CONTINENT.

THE NILE

ASWAN

In 1970, a huge dam was built near Aswan to provide power and control the flooding. Several Ancient Egyptian monuments had to be moved to stop them being submerged by an artificial lake created by the dam.

THEBES

was the capital city of Egypt during the New Kingdom period.

Statue of Ramesses II from the temple at Abu Simbel

ABU SIMBEL

THE NILE WOULD FLOOD EVERY YEAR FROM JUNE TO SEPTEMBER, LEAVING BEHIND HUGE AMOUNTS OF SEDIMENT THAT ALLOWED THE EGYPTIANS TO FARM THE REGION.

EACH YEAR, THE NILE DEPOSITED ABOUT **4 MILLION TONNES** OF NUTRIENT-RICH SEDIMENT – THAT'S THE WEIGHT OF **150 STATUES OF LIBERTY.**

×150

THE WEST BANK OF THE NILE, WHERE THE SUN SETS, WAS LINKED WITH DEATH AND ALL ANCIENT EGYPTIAN TOMBS WERE BUILT ON THIS SIDE OF THE RIVER.

FOOD AND FARMING

The banks of the Nile provided fertile soil for Egyptian farmers to grow enough food to support the entire empire. As well as providing nutrients for the soil and water for the crops, the Nile was also home to a wide range of animals that were hunted for meat and for sport.

THE FARMING YEAR

When the flood waters of the Nile retreated, farmers planted their seeds in the nutrient-rich soil. The season known as Peret was the growing season from October to January, when the farmers tended their crops. When the Nile flooded, farmers repaired their tools and irrigation channels and also helped out with major building projects, including the pyramids.

c.120 days

c.120 days

AKHET
when the
Nile flooded
(June–September)

WEIGHT

Water was carried to the fields by hand or along specially dug **irrigation ditches.** Water was lifted from the channels using large poles with buckets called **shadufs**.

BUCKET

PERET
the growing season
(October–January)

THE THREE MOST IMPORTANT CROPS WERE:

WHEAT TO MAKE FLOUR AND BREAD

FLAX WHICH WAS SPUN TO MAKE LINEN

PAPYRUS WAS USED TO MAKE A PAPER-LIKE PARCHMENT

OTHER CROPS INCLUDED **BARLEY, GRAPES AND DATE PALMS**

HARVEST TIME

Corn was cut down using wooden sickles that had pieces of flint fixed to one edge to make a sharp blade. Once cut, women and children walked behind picking up the ears of corn. Cattle then walked on the corn to separate the grain from the ears. Finally, the grain was tossed in the air, where the wind blew away any remaining unwanted parts of the crop.

The Egyptians divided their year into three seasons:

c.120 days

The rich **topsoil** around the Nile can measure over **20 metres deep** – more than the height of **11 adults** standing on each others' shoulders.

SHEMU
the harvesting season
(February–May)

THE PYRAMIDS

The Egyptians placed great importance on the care of their dead, and important people were buried in lavish tombs. Perhaps the most impressive of these were the pyramids – built to hold the bodies of dead rulers.

SPACE NEEDLE,
SEATTLE, USA
184 M

THE BIGGEST PYRAMIDS

The biggest pyramids are the three at Giza, built for the rulers Khufu, Khafre and Menkaure. The largest, the Pyramid of Khufu, measures 230.4 metres across each side and stood 146.5 metres tall when it was built.

IT WEIGHS NEARLY **6 MILLION TONNES** – 18 TIMES THE WEIGHT OF THE EMPIRE STATE BUILDING.

IT HAS A VOLUME OF ABOUT **2,500,000 CUBIC METRES** – TWICE THAT OF THE HOUSTON ASTRODOME.

ST PAUL'S CATHEDRAL,
LONDON, UK
111 M

PYRAMID OF KHUFU, GIZA, EGYPT

146.5 M

62 M

STEP PYRAMID
SAQQARA, EGYPT

The first pyramid built was the Step Pyramid at Saqqara. It was constructed around 2650 BCE for the Pharaoh Djoser.

INSIDE THE PYRAMID OF KHUFU

Inside the pyramid are three burial chambers, and various tunnels and shafts.

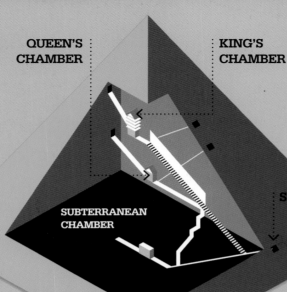

QUEEN'S CHAMBER

KING'S CHAMBER

SHAFT

SUBTERRANEAN CHAMBER

EGYPTOLOGISTS BELIEVE THAT BETWEEN **20,000 AND 30,000 PEOPLE** WERE INVOLVED IN BUILDING THE PYRAMIDS.

IT IS MADE UP OF ABOUT **2.3 MILLION** STONE BLOCKS.

EACH BLOCK WEIGHED UP TO **15 TONNES –** ALMOST THE WEIGHT OF **FOUR ELEPHANTS.**

STONE QUARRY

Some of the stone for the pyramids was cut out of quarries near Aswan and carried more than 900 kilometres up the Nile by boat.

GIZA

EGYPT

ASWAN

The stone blocks were cut with incredible precision – the joints between each block are just 0.5 millimetres wide on average.

130

THE APPROXIMATE NUMBER OF PYRAMIDS DISCOVERED THROUGHOUT EGYPT SO FAR.

230.4 M

TOMBS AND TEMPLES

As well as pyramids, the Egyptians built lavish underground tombs to honour their powerful rulers. They also constructed huge temples in which priests and pharaohs could worship their gods.

HUGE TEMPLE

The mortuary temple of Ramesses III at Medinet Habu, near Luxor, measures about 300 m by 210 m.

300 M

210 M

IT HAS AROUND **7,000** SQUARE METRES OF WALLS DECORATED WITH CARVINGS AND RELIEFS – ENOUGH TO COVER ONE-AND-A-HALF FOOTBALL PITCHES.

GIGANTIC STATUES

Each of the statues of the seated Ramesses II guarding the entrance to his temple at Abu Simbel is 20 metres tall – about three times as tall as a giraffe.

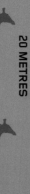

20 METRES

VALLEY OF THE KINGS

During the New Kingdom, Egyptian rulers chose to be buried in an area known as the Valley of the Kings.

NILE

VALLEY OF THE KINGS

LUXOR

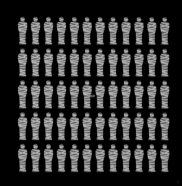

MORE THAN

60

TOMBS HAVE BEEN DISCOVERED SO FAR.

TUTANKHAMUN'S DEATH MASK WEIGHS MORE THAN 10 KG.

PERHAPS THE MOST FAMOUS IS THE TOMB OF **TUTANKHAMUN**. IT WAS FILLED WITH SO MANY ARTEFACTS THAT IT TOOK THE TOMB'S DISCOVERER, **HOWARD CARTER,** 10 YEARS TO CATALOGUE THEM ALL.

IN TOTAL, **5,398** OBJECTS WERE FOUND IN THE TOMB.

BIG GATEWAY

The entrance to a temple was through a huge gateway, known as a pylon. The largest pylon in Egypt forms the gateway to the Temple of Karnak – it is 130 metres wide.

FIRST PYLON, TEMPLE OF KARNAK, NEAR LUXOR

THE TEMPLE AT KARNAK IS ONE OF THE LARGEST RELIGIOUS BUILDINGS EVER CONSTRUCTED. IT COVERS MORE THAN

80 HECTARES –

THREE-AND-A-HALF TIMES THE AREA OF THE US CAPITOL BUILDING IN WASHINGTON, D.C.

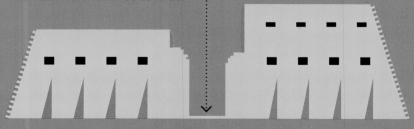

130 M

EGYPTIAN BELIEFS

During their long history, Ancient Egyptians worshipped a wide range of gods and goddesses, including animals such as crocodiles, ibises, bulls, baboons and cats.

ANIMALS WERE SPECIALLY RAISED TO SERVE AS RELIGIOUS SACRIFICES.

ANCIENT EGYPTIANS WORSHIPPED MORE THAN 2,000 GODS AND GODDESSES ...

THOTH
WITH THE HEAD
OF AN IBIS

ANUBIS
WITH THE HEAD
OF A JACKAL

RA/AMON-RA
WITH THE HEAD
OF A HAWK

THE GODS WERE WORSHIPPED BY PRIESTS AND PHARAOHS IN LARGE TEMPLES, WITH OFFERINGS OF FLOWERS, FOOD AND ANIMAL SACRIFICES MADE TO PLEASE THEM.

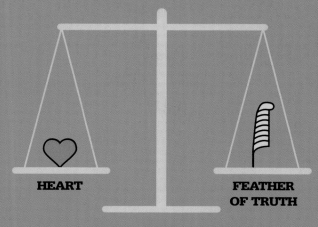

THE FEATHER OF TRUTH

Egyptians believed that after death a person was judged by having their heart weighed against the 'Feather of Truth'. The god Anubis tested the heart and, if it was lighter than the feather, you lived forever. If it was heavier, however, it was eaten by the demon Ammit, who had the head of a crocodile.

SACRED CATS

Cats were sacred animals in Ancient Egypt and most families kept one as a pet to bring good luck. Egyptians could be executed if they killed a cat. Cats were also mummified and buried along with Egyptian dead.

MORE THAN 300,000 MUMMIFIED CATS WERE UNCOVERED BY ARCHAEOLOGISTS IN THE TEMPLE OF BASTET.

... MANY OF WHOM WERE SHOWN WITH THE HEADS OF DIFFERENT ANIMALS.

KHNUM
WITH THE HEAD OF A
CURLY-HORNED RAM

SOBEK
WITH THE HEAD
OF A CROCODILE

THE GENERAL PUBLIC WAS NOT ALLOWED INSIDE THE TEMPLES AND THEY ONLY CAME INTO CONTACT WITH THEIR GODS WHEN RELIGIOUS STATUES WERE PARADED OUTSIDE DURING RELIGIOUS PROCESSIONS.

DURING THE REIGN OF THE PHARAOH AKHENATEN, WHO RULED AROUND 1351–1334 BCE, WORSHIP OF THE TRADITIONAL GODS WAS ABOLISHED AND REPLACED WITH THE WORSHIP OF THE SUN, KNOWN AS THE ATEN.

THE AFTERLIFE

After their death, important Egyptians were preserved in a process called mummification and buried with various goods and objects. The Egyptians believed that these would be useful in the afterlife.

EYE OF HORUS

Objects buried with the dead included amulets, such as the Eye of Horus to ward off evil, and small statues of people, which would come to life when called by the dead person and serve them in the afterlife.

HOW TO MAKE A MUMMY

1. Wash the body with water and a type of salt called natron.

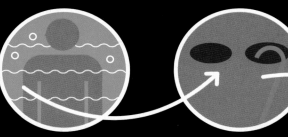

2. Push a hook through the nose and use it to break up the brain.

5. Cut down the left side of the body and pull out the internal organs.

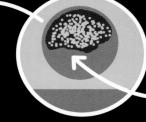

4. Fill the empty skull with sawdust.

3. Pull the bits of the brain out using the hook.

6. Treat the organs with natron salt and place them in canopic jars to go in the tomb.

7. Clean the body with palm wine and spices and pack it with straw.

8. Place the body on a sloping table and cover it with salt to dry out over 40 days.

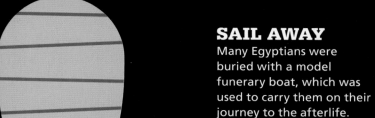

SAIL AWAY

Many Egyptians were buried with a model funerary boat, which was used to carry them on their journey to the afterlife.

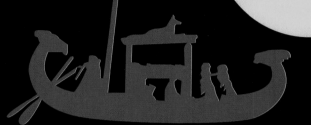

OTHER OBJECTS FOUND BURIED INCLUDED **FURNITURE**, **POTTERY**, AND **CASKETS**.

AN EGYPTIAN MUMMY WAS WRAPPED IN ABOUT

1.6 KM OF LINEN FABRIC ...

... **ENOUGH TO GO AROUND AN ATHLETICS TRACK FOUR TIMES.**

×4

THE LINEN COVERED AN AREA OF ABOUT 375 SQUARE METRES – ENOUGH TO COVER ONE-AND-A-HALF TENNIS COURTS.

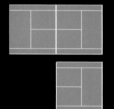

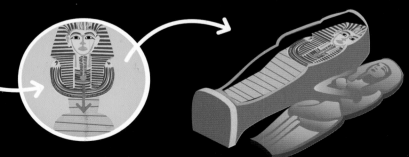

9. Now wrap the entire body in linen fabric.

10. Cover the face with a death mask.

11. Place the body in a sarcophagus.

EGYPTIAN SOCIETY

Egyptian society was a strict hierarchy, with the pharaoh and his court at the top and farmers and slaves at the bottom. Each layer of society had its own particular role and range of responsibilities.

VIZIER

The pharaoh's top adviser, he controlled the administration and was responsible for the distribution of food and running the royal court.

NOBLES

The nobles ruled the regions of Egypt, known as nomes. They kept order in their region and upheld local laws.

SCRIBES

These kept records about everything in the empire, from the amount of food produced to the size of the army and how many workers were employed.

CRAFTSMEN

Pottery makers, sculptors, painters, weavers and leatherworkers often worked in groups in special workshops.

FARMERS

These worked the land for the pharaoh and were given homes, food and clothes in return.

THE PHARAOH

The ruler was believed to be a god, making laws and keeping order throughout the empire. He kept the gods happy and made sure that the empire was safe from invasion.

PRIESTS

These performed rituals in their temples to keep the gods happy.

WOMEN RULERS

The role of pharaoh usually passed from father to son, but several women became rulers, including Hatshepsut and Cleopatra. Some chose to wear the trappings of a male king, including a false beard.

SOLDIERS

Soldiers fought enemies of the empire and could be rewarded with a share of any captured riches as well as land.

SLAVES

Slaves were usually prisoners who had been captured during wars. They worked in households as well as mines and quarries.

THE PHARAOH

The pharaoh was the ultimate ruler in Ancient Egypt, the controller of all power throughout the empire, and worshipped as a god on Earth.

The **blue headdress, or nemes,** was a striped headcloth that covered the head and neck.

The word 'pharaoh' means 'great house'.

These glyphs spell out 'great house'.

ARM BAND

Pharaohs were often portrayed wearing a **false beard.**

LONG STAFF

The pharaoh usually carried two symbols of his authority, the **crook** and the **flail.**

170
The approximate number of pharaohs who ruled Egypt.

These were split into more than 30 groups, known as dynasties.

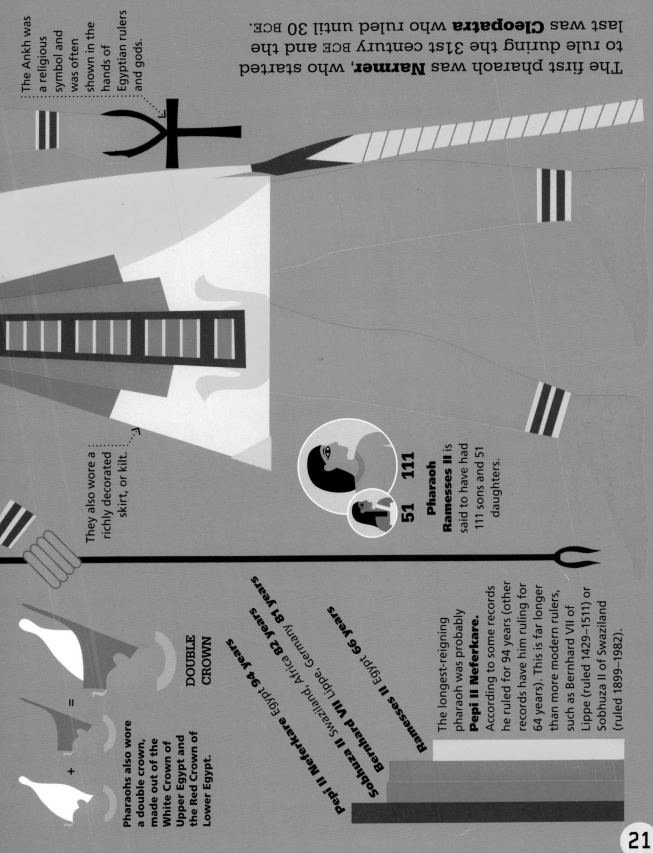

The Ankh was a religious symbol and was often shown in the hands of Egyptian rulers and gods.

The first Pharaoh was **Narmer**, who started to rule during the 31st century BCE and the last was **Cleopatra** who ruled until 30 BCE.

They also wore a richly decorated skirt, or kilt.

Pharaoh **Ramesses II** is said to have had 111 sons and 51 daughters.

51 111

DOUBLE CROWN

Pharaohs also wore a double crown, made out of the White Crown of Upper Egypt and the Red Crown of Lower Egypt.

Pepi II Neferkare Egypt **94 years**

Sobhuza II Swaziland, Africa **82 years**

Bernhard VII Lippe, Germany **81 years**

Ramesses II Egypt **66 years**

The longest-reigning pharaoh was probably **Pepi II Neferkare.**

According to some records he ruled for 94 years (other records have him ruling for 64 years). This is far longer than more modern rulers, such as Bernhard VII of Lippe (ruled 1429–1511) or Sobhuza II of Swaziland (ruled 1899–1982).

EGYPTIAN WARFARE

At its height, Ancient Egypt ruled a huge area of northern Africa and the Middle East. This region was controlled with the help of a powerful army and naval forces who protected trade routes and set out to defeat troublesome neighbours.

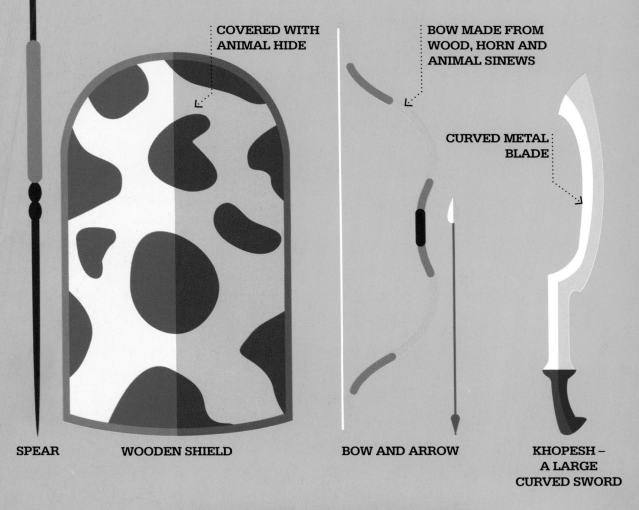

COVERED WITH ANIMAL HIDE

BOW MADE FROM WOOD, HORN AND ANIMAL SINEWS

CURVED METAL BLADE

SPEAR

WOODEN SHIELD

BOW AND ARROW

KHOPESH –
A LARGE
CURVED SWORD

EGYPTIAN WEAPONS

EGYPTIAN WARSHIP

An Egyptian warship had a single mast, which held a large, square sail. There were also about 50 rowers to propel the vessel. Each ship weighed about 70–80 tonnes – as much as 20 hippos. The bow usually had a decoration of a lion's head crushing a human skull. These ships were used to carry troops, as a platform for archers to shoot from, and to sink enemy ships.

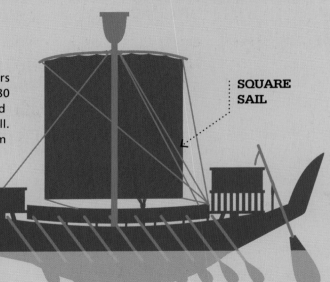

SQUARE SAIL

LION'S HEAD

BATTLE OF KADESH

Fought in 1274 BCE, the battle saw the Egyptians fight the Hittites, with both sides claiming victory.

1 Column of Egyptian army in four groups.

Hittite camp

Egyptian army

2 Hittite forces surprised the second group and rounded on the isolated first group.

Hittite forces

3 The first group was saved when Ne'arin allies arrived, forcing Hittites to flee.

Ne'arin allies

Chariots were introduced by the Hyksos when they conquered and ruled Egypt around 1650 BCE.

Chariots had a driver who held the reins and a whip to drive the horses, and a fighter who was armed with a bow and arrows as well as several spears to use when all the arrows had been shot.

In battle, chariots were used in groups known as troops, squadrons and pedjets.

TROOP 10

 =10 chariots

SQUADRON 50

PEDJET 250

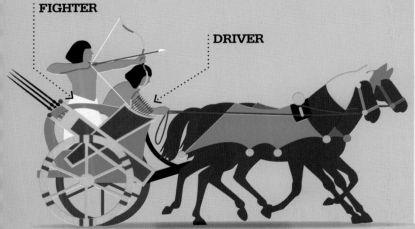

FIGHTER

DRIVER

WRITING AND LANGUAGE

The Egyptians used a system of small pictures called hieroglyphs to write down their language. These images represented letters, sounds or even whole words, and they covered the walls of tombs, temples, palaces and sheets of a paper-like material called papyrus. However, their meaning remained a mystery for thousands of years, until a chance discovery by a French scholar.

3000 BCE The date the Egyptians developed the hieroglyph system.

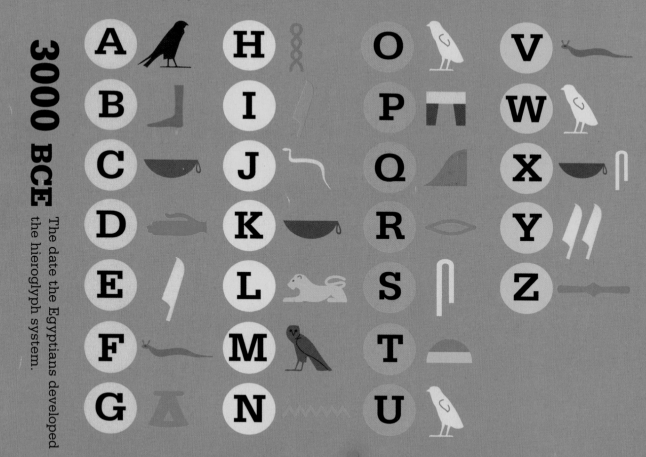

The word **hieroglyph** comes from two Greek words: **hieros** meaning 'holy' and **glyphe** meaning 'writing'.

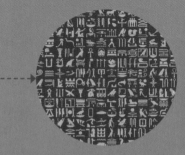

The number of hieroglyphs expanded from about **800** during the Old Kingdom period to more than **5,000** during the Ptolemaic and Roman periods.

The names of kings and queens were written inside oval-shaped boxes called cartouches.

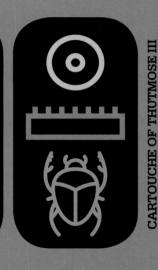

CARTOUCHE OF THUTMOSE III

The Egyptians recorded much of their information on papyrus.

Workers cut and gather the stalks of the papyrus plant.

They peel off the outer layer and cut the middle of the stem into thin strips.

The strips are laid out horizontally and vertically, covered with a cloth and beaten with a mallet.

Once dry, the papyrus is rubbed smooth with a stone and written on using a pen made from a reed.

ROSETTA STONE

People could not translate hieroglyphs until the discovery of the Rosetta Stone. In 1822, a French scholar called Jean-François Champollion realised it contained the same text in Egyptian hieroglyphs, Demotic script (a common Egyptian language) and Ancient Greek. Champollion was able to use these other known languages to crack the secret of the unknown hieroglyphs.

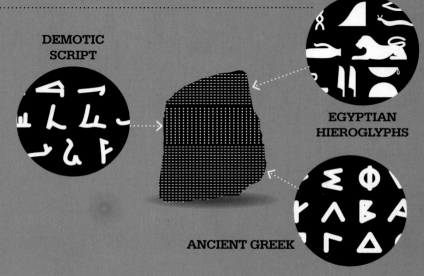

DEMOTIC SCRIPT

EGYPTIAN HIEROGLYPHS

ANCIENT GREEK

CRAFTS AND CULTURE

Egyptian craftsmen were highly skilled and worked with a wide range of materials from stone to metal to pigments. They created huge buildings, make-up and intricate jewellery, and board games to entertain people.

SENET BOARD GAME

The Egyptians played a board game called Senet. The game dates back to about 3500 BCE and it was played on a long board with 30 squares. Players had several pieces which they moved around the board according to the roll of dice or throwing sticks.

Ptah, the **god of wisdom** and one of the gods that created the world, was the **patron god of craftsmen** in Ancient Egypt.

Egyptians believed that the make-up they wore had healing powers. Both men and women wore make-up, especially a dark substance called kohl, which was applied around the eyes.

The world's first industrial strike occurred in the village of Deir el-Medina in 1153 BCE. Craftsmen held a sit-in outside royal funerary temples to protest that they hadn't been paid the wheat and barley promised in return for the work they had done.

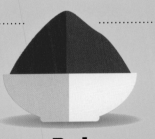

Egyptian artists would practise drawing using small pieces of pottery or limestone, known as **ostraca.**

The Egyptians created coloured pigments using various naturally occurring substances.

Yellow
OCHRE

Red
IRON OXIDE

Green
MALACHITE

White
LIME AND GYPSUM

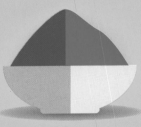

Blue
COPPER CARBONATE

WHAT HAPPENED NEXT?

There are many possible reasons why the Egyptian empire collapsed, some of which date back more than a thousand years before its eventual decline. They include power and wealth being controlled by a small elite, the influence of foreign soldiers and the overstretching of the region's valuable but limited resources.

TANIS

THEBES

1069 BCE

DIVISION

At the end of the New Kingdom, a split occurred and the country divided into two states around 1069 BCE, with one ruled from Thebes and the other from Tanis.

30%

THE PRIESTS

The power of priests meant that they controlled a huge area of Egypt – up to 30 per cent of the empire. This left little for the rest of the people to farm and feed themselves.

AROUND 525 BCE, THE POWERFUL **PERSIAN EMPIRE** TOOK CONTROL OF EGYPT. EVEN THOUGH EGYPTIANS RESTORED RULE FOR A BRIEF PERIOD, THERE WAS SO MUCH IN-FIGHTING AND SQUABBLING THAT THE PERSIANS QUICKLY CONQUERED THE STATE AGAIN.

ALEXANDER

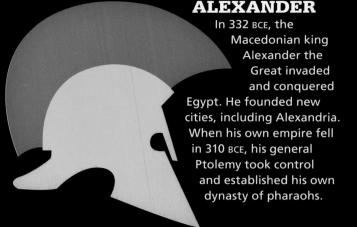

In 332 BCE, the Macedonian king Alexander the Great invaded and conquered Egypt. He founded new cities, including Alexandria. When his own empire fell in 310 BCE, his general Ptolemy took control and established his own dynasty of pharaohs.

In 30 BCE, the last pharaoh died, when **Cleopatra VII** killed herself following defeat to the Roman army. After that, Egypt became a province of Rome.

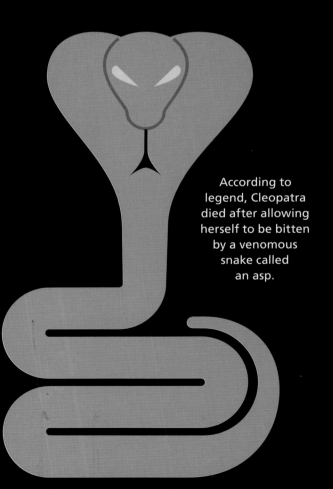

According to legend, Cleopatra died after allowing herself to be bitten by a venomous snake called an asp.

ACCORDING TO SOME SOURCES, EGYPT SUPPLIED AS MUCH AS

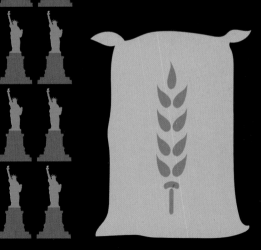

420,000 TONNES

OF GRAIN TO THE ROMAN EMPIRE EVERY YEAR ...

... THAT'S **17 TIMES** THE WEIGHT OF THE STATUE OF LIBERTY.

GLOSSARY

afterlife
The period after a person has died.

amulet
A piece of jewellery that is said to protect a person from evil.

canopic jar
A special container that was used to hold the body parts of a mummy.

capital city
The main city of a country where the rulers govern from.

crook
A stick with a curved hook at one end, which was used as a symbol of the pharaoh's power.

cartouche
An oblong or oval shape containing the characters and glyphs of an Egyptian ruler or god.

death mask
The mask placed over the head of a mummy.

delta
The point where a river meets the sea and drops any sediment it is carrying, creating a fan of channels in a triangular shape.

dynasty
A sequence of rulers who usually belong to the same family.

flail
An object used to thresh grain and also as a weapon. It was also a symbol of the pharaoh's power.

funerary temple
Also called a mortuary temple, this was a place of worship that was built next to a royal tomb and designed to celebrate that ruler's life.

hierarchy
A system where people and objects are organised in a graded order.

hieroglyphs
A system of pictures used to represent letters, sounds and even entire words.

ibis
A wading bird with a long curving bill.

irrigation
The supplying of water to crops.

kohl
A dark powder that was used as make-up, especially around the eyes.

Lower Egypt
The northernmost part of Egypt situated largely around the Nile Delta.

mummification
Preserving the remains of a dead person.

oasis
An area of a desert where water reaches the surface, creating a fertile spot.

ostraca
Pieces of broken pottery which Egyptian artists used to practise writing and drawing on.

papyrus
A tall plant which grows on the banks of rivers and which the Egyptians used to make a form of paper, also called papyrus.

pharaoh
The name given to Ancient Egyptian rulers.

pylon
In Ancient Egypt, this was the name given to the huge entrances to temples.

quarry
A place where stone is dug out of the ground.

sacrifice
To give something up or kill something or someone, often as part of a religious ceremony.

sarcophagus
A large stone coffin or tomb.

sediment
Mud, earth and rocks that are carried by a river from one place and dropped at another.

topsoil
The surface layer of soil.

Upper Egypt
Part of Ancient Egypt south of the Nile Delta.

vizier
A senior official in Ancient Egypt.

pyramid
A building made from four triangle-shaped sides that meet in a point at the top.

Websites

MORE INFO:
www.historyforkids.net/ancient-egypt.html
A website that's packed full of information about what life was like in Ancient Egypt.

egypt.mrdonn.org
This website is teeming with information about Ancient Egypt, including its rulers, people, religion and technology.

www.childrensuniversity.manchester.ac.uk/interactives/history/egypt/
Set up by the University of Manchester, this site is devoted to all things from Ancient Egypt.

MORE GRAPHICS:
www.visualinformation.info
A website that contains a whole host of infographic material on subjects as diverse as natural history, science and sport.

www.coolinfographics.com
A collection of infographics and data visualisations from other online resources, magazines and newspapers.

www.dailyinfographic.com
A comprehensive collection of infographics on an enormous range of topics that is updated every single day!

INDEX

ACKNOWLEDGEMENTS

Published in Great Britain
in 2018 by Wayland
Copyright © Hodder and Stoughton Ltd, 2016
All rights reserved

Editor: Elizabeth Brent
Produced by Tall Tree Ltd
Editor: Jon Richards
Designer: Jonathan Vipond

ISBN: 978 0 7502 9187 3
10 9 8 7 6 5 4 3 2 1

Wayland
An imprint of Hachette
Children's Group
Part of Hodder and Stoughton
Carmelite House
50 Victoria Embankment
London EC4Y 0DZ

An Hachette UK Company
www.hachette.co.uk
www.hachettechildrens.co.uk

Printed and bound in China

The website addresses (URLs) included in this
book were valid at the time of going to press.
However, it is possible that contents or
addresses may have changed since the
publication of this book. No responsibility
for any such changes can be accepted by
either the author or the Publisher.